Understanding Investment and the Stock Market

By
KARL BIEDENWEG, Ph.D

COPYRIGHT © 2003 Mark Twain Media, Inc.

ISBN 1-58037-226-0

Printing No. CD-1572

Mark Twain Media, Inc., Publishers
Distributed by Carson-Dellosa Publishing Company, Inc.

Table of Contents

Introduction

This easy-to-read book will introduce the beginning investor to the basics of investing in the stock market. First, we will discuss some of the **vehicles** (stocks, bonds, T-bills, mutual funds) from which an investor can choose. Next, we will look at the history of the stock markets and learn the basics about how they work. Then, we will look at how to evaluate our different investment options, along with how and why we should **diversify** (invest in more than one investment vehicle).

Included in this book are puzzles, games, and worksheets to reinforce learning. Extension activities that encourage students to conduct further research allow them to reach beyond the classroom to increase their understanding of the financial world. Directions for a stock market trading game are also included. There is a glossary of frequently used financial terms in the back of the book for easy reference.

Like anything else worthwhile in life, investing takes knowledge, practice, and a pinch of good luck. Invest in yourself and in your future.

A Quick Overview of Investing

What is an investment?

When money is put into some tangible item or financial instrument for the purpose of increasing an original amount of money, an **investment** has been made. An investment can be made in many different ways, such as buying land, antiques, gold, cattle, bonds, fine artworks, or stocks, or money can be put into bank accounts. When money is used to purchase any of these items in the hope of creating more money, then an investment has taken place.

How are investments made?

Regardless of where a person decides to invest money, there are a few basic steps in the process that are worth reviewing before we plunge ahead. First, an investor must decide how he or she wishes to invest his or her money. Many investors choose stocks, bonds, or other financial instruments for two very good reasons.

First, stocks and bonds are considered to be **liquid assets**. This means that stocks and bonds, in most cases, can be easily sold when the investor is ready to sell. If you put your money into a piece of fine art or a herd of goats, for example, there may not be another investor who is ready to buy it when the time comes.

Second, the rate of return, or profit, is often "promised" before money is put into an investment. In the case of a bank account, an interest rate is promised by the bank. In other words, the bank pays the investor a fixed amount to keep his money in a bank account. Some companies pay investors interest to own stocks (called dividends). In this way, some of the uncertainty is removed before an investor commits his or her money to an investment. The investor has an idea of what to expect before the investment has even been made.

At some point, the investment must be sold in order for the investor to make a profit. This can happen in a variety of ways, depending on where an investor has put his or her money. It may be as easy as cashing in a bank account, sending a rare work of art to be sold at an auction house, or selling stocks through a stock exchange.

More information will follow on exactly how stocks and bonds are sold, but the process can be as easy as calling a stockbroker or placing a sell order online with a computer.

Name: _____ Date: _____

A Quick Overview of Investing (cont.)

What causes an investment to go up (or down) in value?

Many factors can influence the value of an investment. Most investments are determined by the simple economic principle of supply and demand. For most goods, the price of the item goes up as the supply gets lower. A simple example would be that of a popular toy during the holiday season. Once the limited supply of that toy sells out at the retail store, you'll often see it offered for sale in the newspaper classifieds or online auctions at a much higher price. Scarcity has caused the price of this item to rise sharply. Likewise, after the holiday season is over and the toy stores are able to re-stock this popular item, the price will return to normal, since many are readily available.

Since a share of stock is basically a tiny ownership stake in a particular company, stocks work somewhat like the simplified toy example. The main difference is that many things affect the price of a stock. What type of product does the company produce? How good are they at competing with other companies that are in the same line of business? How much money does this company earn, and what are its profits? The answers to these questions help determine the price of a particular company's stock.

Since so many factors can contribute to a stock's price, predicting the future value of a stock can be a risky business for the investor. Keep in mind that putting money into an investment does not always ensure that a profit will be made for the investor. Sometimes investments lose money.

Questions to Consider

1. Would loaning a friend $10 to buy a movie ticket be considered an investment? Why or why not?

   _____

   _____

   _____

2. If a person invested $10,000 to start a small computer repair service but lost most of that money in the first three months, would this be considered an investment? Why or why not?

   _____

   _____

   _____

3. Why do you think it is important to so many investors to invest in liquid assets, things that can readily be turned into cash, such as stocks, bonds, or bank accounts?

   _____

   _____

   _____

Name: _____ Date: _____

A Quick Overview of Investing (cont.)

4. Why would buying an antique automobile probably be a poor choice as an investment for most people when compared to simply opening a bank savings account?

   _____

   _____

   _____

5. Imagine that you have made an investment by buying one of only five known autographs of a famous musician who lived during the 1700s. Shortly afterward, you hear that an auction house has just announced the discovery of 200 pieces of sheet music with this same musician's authentic signature on each piece. What would you expect to happen to the value of your investment?

   _____

   _____

   _____

6. If a company makes an excellent product that you enjoy using, should it follow that the company's stock would make an excellent investment? Why or why not?

   _____

   _____

   _____

7. Do you think the price of an investment can be affected by the way people might feel about that investment, as opposed to the investment's real underlying value? Explain your position.

   _____

   _____

   _____

8. What kinds of questions would you ask of someone offering you the opportunity to invest money in an idea, product, or company?

   _____

   _____

   _____

Name: _____ Date: _____

Using Financial Terms

Directions: Understanding financially related language is one of the biggest hurdles to learning how certain financial markets work. For this activity, use the word choices below to best complete or match each sentence. Use a dictionary or the Internet if you need help with these terms. Choices will only be used once, and some will not be used.

margin buying	stock index	dollar cost averaging
investment	cost basis	day trading
commission	short sell	diversification
risk	stock	interest
municipal bond	dividend	blue chip stock
junk bond	bears/bulls	mutual fund
treasuries	P/E ratio	

1. A/an _____ is money put into a financial instrument or tangible item for the purpose of increasing the original amount of money.

2. A share of ownership in a company. _____

3. Percentage amount paid by banks or other financial institutions on monetary deposits. _____

4. _____ gives a figure for the overall price paid for a block of stock.

5. Special kind of bond that carries a higher interest payment since the company's credit worthiness is not highly rated. _____

6. Financial instruments issued by the U.S. government. _____

7. A/an _____ is a small payment given to the shareholder as a reward for holding a company's stock.

8. An investor who strongly favors a buy and hold strategy would find much to disagree with in this strategy. _____

9. A/an _____ is a large stock portfolio where many investors have pooled their money.

10. _____ allows investors a way to determine the per share price of stock they own, even though it may have been purchased at different price levels.

Name: _____ Date: _____

Using Financial Terms (cont.)

11. A/an _____ is a numerical method for tracking many stocks to easily gauge how a larger market is doing.

12. _____ is a strategy that calls for borrowing money against stock holdings in order to buy more stock.

13. Fee paid to a broker for handling a stock transaction. _____

14. Splitting investments into different areas to avoid the harmful effect of losses in a single area.

    _____

15. _____

    is a primary factor in selecting an investment, since it determines how well the investment should pay, as well as how much threat there is to the monies invested.

16. Strategy used by an investor to make money in stocks that are in decline.

    _____

Section I: Investment Options

Chapter 1: Investment Vehicles

"To the man who only has a hammer in the tool kit, every problem looks like a nail."

— Abraham Maslow

A vehicle is something you use to get from where you are now to where you want to be. For example, if you wanted to go shopping at the mall, you might ride the bus, train, or taxi, or have a friend or relative drive you. There are pros and cons associated with each of your transportation **options** (vehicles). One vehicle might be faster than another, one vehicle might be safer than the rest, or another vehicle might be cheaper than the others. You need to use the vehicle that is right for your current situation.

When we invest in the stock market, we usually do so with a financial goal in mind. This goal, whether short-term or long-term, is where we want to be in the future. A **short-term goal** might be to save enough money for a down payment on a house; a **long-term goal** might be to retire financially secure. Let's take a closer look at the most common **investment vehicles** (common stocks, bonds, T-bills, mutual funds) we can use to reach our goals.

7

Chapter 2: Banks and Simple Interest

Bank accounts that pay interest are considered among the safest forms of investments. Deposits are insured by the Federal Deposit Insurance Corporation (FDIC), and investors have little worry that money invested in a savings account will be lost. In this way, the interest paid by banks forms the baseline by which other investments must be measured. Why would an investor risk his or her money in a particular investment unless the return on that investment is enough to walk away from the safety of a guaranteed interest-paying bank account?

One of the first questions an investor needs to ask when considering an investment is: Am I being adequately rewarded in return for the risk being assumed on this investment? That's why understanding how interest works on bank deposits is necessary before an investor can reasonably consider the risk/reward offered by other investments.

We'll take a look at **simple interest** in this activity. The formula for computing simple interest is

Interest Rate x Principal = Interest Earned

In this formula, **principal** simply means the amount of money invested.

Example:

A. Lyle deposited $5,000 into a savings account. The account pays 5% interest per year. How much money will Lyle earn from this investment at the end of the one-year term?

   $5,000 x 5% = Interest Earned
   $5,000 x   0.05 = $250

Lyle's deposit will earn $250 in interest the first year. This means that at the end of 1 year, his account would have a balance of $5,250, once the interest has been added to his beginning balance.

B. Beverly invested $12,800 in a one-year certificate of deposit at her bank. Interest on this certificate is 6.6%. How much money will her investment have earned when the CD matures?

   $12,800 x 6.6% = Interest Earned
   $12,800 x 0.066 = $844.80

This CD will earn $844.80 at maturity.

Name: _____ Date: _____

Chapter 2: Banks and Simple Interest (cont.)

Directions: Answer each of the following questions regarding the computation of simple interest.

1. How much interest will be earned at the end of one year on a deposit of $340 in an account that pays 2.9% annual interest?

   _____

2. Stacy was given a gift of $4,000 from her grandparents. If she deposits the money in her savings account, it will earn 4.45% interest per year. How much will she have earned in interest on this money at the end of one year?

   _____

3. An investor, worried about the ups and downs of the stock market, decided to park $125,000 in a bank certificate of deposit paying 8.8% interest. How much money will the investor have at the end of the year in principal, plus interest earned?

   _____

4. John sold some company stock that paid dividends, opting instead for a bank account that offered 4.75% annual interest. He deposited $48,200 in this account. How much interest can he expect to earn on this account at the end of one year?

   _____

5. Maureen was considering a risky investment, which a friend has promised will earn 14.5% interest in the first year. She now has her $20,000 in a bank account that pays 2.75% interest. Her friend is trying to convince Maureen to invest the money by showing her the difference between what the two investments will earn. How much more will the risky investment earn than the bank account, assuming it goes as expected?

   _____

6. Gene was thinking of investing $10,000 with a bank near his house at 3.25% interest. It's convenient for Gene to go to this branch, even though another bank across town is offering 3.65% interest on the same kind of account. How much will Gene lose in interest in one year if he deposits his money in the bank offering the lower interest rate?

   _____

7. Paul earned 12.75% interest on a $6,500 investment for putting the money at risk for only one month. With this money, a friend of his started a restaurant, which immediately became popular. Paul is thinking of putting his original investment, plus the interest he earned, into another investment. How much money does Paul have to invest?

   _____

Chapter 3: Common Stock

The ownership of a corporation is divided into **transferable** units known as shares of stock. There are several categories, or classes, of stock. Individuals and companies buy stocks because they expect to **profit** when the corporation makes profits. Corporations issue two basic types of stock: **common stock** and **preferred stock**.

Corporations differ from other types of business structures, such as sole proprietorships and partnerships. In sole proprietorships, one person (the owner) receives the profits. In partnerships, only the partners share in any financial gains. But in a corporation, hundreds, thousands, and sometimes even millions, of stockholders share the profits. Furthermore, in the corporate **structure**, stockholders may buy and sell ownership (company stock) without interfering with the activities of the corporation. There are millions of **transactions** that occur daily on stock exchanges, and they are independent transactions between buyers and sellers that do not affect the daily operations of the corporations involved. This is in contrast to sole proprietorships and partnerships, where the life of the business **ceases** when **ownership** changes.

Sole Proprietorship   Partnership   Corporation

One other important distinction between a corporation and the other types of business structures is **investors** (stockholders) in a corporation limit their losses to the amount that they invest in shares of stock, if the company would get into serious financial difficulties.

The most popular investment vehicle in the stock market is **common stock**. One share of common stock represents one-part ownership in a corporation. If you owned 1,000 common shares of ABC Corporation, and they have 100,000 shares **outstanding** (sold), then you would own 1% of the ABC Corporation. As a **shareholder** (owner), you have the right to vote on important corporate issues, such as the election of a corporation's board of directors, and **mergers or acquisitions** (the joining with, or the taking over of, another company).

There are two basic ways that an investor can make money by buying common stock. The first way is that the stock could increase in market value. The stock price will increase in market

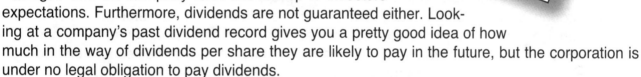

Chapter 3: Common Stock (cont.)

value when buyers bid the stock price up when trying to acquire shares of the stock. You, no doubt, have seen this happen with other consumer products. When the PlayStation 2™ Video Game System first came out, everybody wanted one, but there were not enough systems available; thus, people were willing to pay more than the suggested retail price in order to acquire the system. While game players were trying to acquire the system, investors were trying to acquire Sony (the manufacturer) stock. Those investors who currently held Sony stock could sell to those trying to acquire the stock at a price higher than the price they originally paid for the stock, thus making a profit.

The second way of making money via common stock is through the corporation's dividend policy. A **dividend** is money given to each shareholder as a way of sharing the corporate profits with the owners or stockholders. Typically, the more profit a corporation makes, the more dividends the stockholders make.

It should be noted at this point that making money by investing in common stock is not guaranteed. The market price of the stock could drop in value if the company is mismanaged or if the company does not live up to investors' expectations. Furthermore, dividends are not guaranteed either. Looking at a company's past dividend record gives you a pretty good idea of how much in the way of dividends per share they are likely to pay in the future, but the corporation is under no legal obligation to pay dividends.

A distinctive feature of corporations is that they have shares of stock, and they can distribute profits to the shareholders via dividends. The dividends that are paid to shareholders represent a positive return on investment (profit) for the firm and can be directly distributed to the shareholders. As mentioned above, the payment of dividends is at the discretion (option) of the board of directors. Some important characteristics of dividends include the following:

- Unless the board of directors of the corporation declares a dividend, it is not a liability of the corporation. A corporation cannot default on an undeclared dividend. As a consequence, corporations cannot become bankrupt because of nonpayment of an undeclared dividend.

- The payment of dividends by the corporation is not a business expense. Dividends are not tax deductible for corporations.

- Dividends received by individual shareholders are, for the most part, considered ordinary income by the IRS, and are fully taxable.

"Bulls make money. Bears make money. Pigs get slaughtered."
— Anonymous

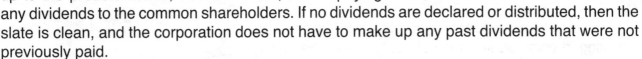

Chapter 4: Preferred Stock

Preferred stock has attained this name because it receives preferential treatment when it comes to the payment of dividends. Not all companies have preferred stock. But for those that do, they need to pay a predetermined, stated amount of dividend to the preferred shareholders before they can distribute any dividends to common shareholders.

Dividend payments are not legally required; thus, if the company does not have excess profits, it might very well forgo paying dividends that year. This leads us to the different types of preferred stock. The two major classes of preferred stock are **non-cumulative** and **cumulative**.

Non-cumulative preferred stock requires the corporation to first pay dividends to the preferred shareholder, up to the predetermined, stated amount, before paying any dividends to the common shareholders. If no dividends are declared or distributed, then the slate is clean, and the corporation does not have to make up any past dividends that were not previously paid.

Cumulative preferred stock also requires the corporation to pay preferred shareholders before common shareholders. But with cumulative preferred stock, any unpaid past dividends must be brought up-to-date before any dividends can be paid to common stock shareholders. It might seem like purchasing preferred stock makes a lot more sense than purchasing common stock, because preferred shareholders always get paid first. While preferred shareholders do

get paid first, they only get the predetermined, stated amount of dividend and never any more than that. Thus, if the company is doing very well, then the common shareholders are likely to receive much larger dividends than preferred shareholders. Usually, the preferred stock dividend is much smaller than common stock dividends, and the market price of preferred stock is much more stable than common stock. Your **risk tolerance** (how much you're willing to lose compared to how much you would like to gain) will be a big factor in choosing the type of stock you purchase.

Preferred stock also differs from common stock in that it usually does not have voting rights on important corporate matters, as does common stock.

"A market is the combined behavior of thousands of people responding to information, misinformation, and whim."

— Kenneth Chang

Chapter 4: Common and Preferred Stock–Activities

Guest Speaker

Have a local stock broker come to class and further explain stocks and the marketplace. Also, have the broker explain how to read the stock reports in *The Wall Street Journal*.

Student Activities

1. A corporation has 1,000 shares of preferred stock and 5,000 shares of common stock, and the preferred stock has a prior claim to an annual $5 dividend. The annual profits to be distributed over the first three years were $15,000, $25,000, and $4,000, respectively. Calculate how much would be distributed to preferred stock and common stock. Also, calculate the dividends per share.

Distribution	First Year	Second Year	Third Year
Preferred Stock	_____	_____	_____
Common Stock	_____	_____	_____

Dividend Per Share			
Preferred Stock	_____	_____	_____
Common Stock	_____	_____	_____

2. A corporation has 1,000 shares of preferred stock and 4,000 shares of common stock. The preferred stock has a prior claim to an annual $8 dividend. If the annual profits to be distributed for the first three years were $20,000, $35,000, and $60,000, respectively, how much would be distributed to preferred stock and common stock? Also, calculate the dividends per share.

Distribution	First Year	Second Year	Third Year
Preferred Stock	_____	_____	_____
Common Stock	_____	_____	_____

Dividend Per Share			
Preferred Stock	_____	_____	_____
Common Stock	_____	_____	_____

Chapter 5: Stock Purchases and Cost Basis

In recent years, many investors have opened online accounts with brokerage firms, and they buy and sell stocks using a computer. However, these buy and sell orders are still placed by the brokerage company, and a fee is charged to the investor for this service. The fee is called a **commission**. These online transactions are typically the least expensive way to buy or sell stocks, since a live person is not required to deal with the customer directly in order for the trade to be processed.

Many investors still call their broker via telephone to place a buy or sell order. Typically, these transactions cost more in commissions, especially if the broker is providing advice on which stocks to buy or sell. The cost of dealing with a broker in this manner may be many times the amount of an online trade.

Once the investor has either logged on to his or her brokerage account or called his or her broker, the investor receives information about the current price of a stock. If the investor considers that the price being quoted for a stock meets his or her own investment goals, then a buy or sell order might be given at that time.

Since the price of a stock often fluctuates, the price quote the investor is given by his or her broker, or the price quote they saw online may not be the same as the price at which the actual transaction occurs. For instance, the shares of a particular company may be shown at $22.50, but by the time the customer hits the place-order button on his computer, perhaps the price has ticked up to $23. Perhaps it has dropped to $22.25. This reflects the auction-like atmosphere of the stock trading floor. Sometimes, though, these price bumps represent manipulations by shrewd stock players who make money by buying and selling a particular stock many times during the day.

Example:

An investor calls his broker and places an order to buy 100 shares of a company. The price quoted is $40 per share. The commission charged by this particular broker for this kind of transaction is $50.

Bought 100 shares at $40 per share = $4,000

Commission charged $ 50

Total cost of this block of shares was $4,050

The **cost basis per share** is found by dividing $4,050 (total cost) by 100 (number of shares bought). The cost basis per share on this transaction was $40.50. Knowing the cost basis per share can be important when large blocks of stock are bought and then sold in smaller blocks over a period of time.

You can see from this example that the price of the stock would need to go up beyond $40.50 for the investor to make money by selling this stock. Considering that there will be a commission charged when they go to sell the stock, the price of this stock would need to be over $41 per share for the investor to make any money, if he pays the same commission fee on the sale of the stock.

Name: _____   Date: _____

Chapter 5: Stock Purchases and Cost Basis (cont.)

Directions: Answer the following questions concerning total cost and cost basis per share.

1. Amy purchased 80 shares of a company's stock for $14.25 per share, paying an online commission of $16 for the purchase. What was her total cost for this block of shares?

    _____

2. Stuart called his broker to take advantage of a hot stock tip he overheard at the coffee-house that morning. His broker charges Stuart $65 to place a stock order. The 50 shares that Stuart wanted were purchased at $84 per share. What was his total cost for this block of shares?

    _____

3. Barney manages a small mutual fund on behalf of his relatives. He wishes that he did not, however, since the relatives are constantly breathing down his neck about the decisions he makes. He purchased 2,500 shares of a company for $18.75 per share, paying a commission of $225. His cousin Bernie has already phoned, wanting to know what the cost basis per share is for this block of stock. What is the cost basis per share for this stock?

    _____

4. Arthur's broker was running a $6 special rate commission on the purchase of stocks recommended by the brokerage house. Arthur was aware that some unscrupulous brokers might push a particular company stock and use such a special commission deal to induce investors to buy shares of a loser. However, Arthur is convinced that his broker is trying to put him into some good stock deals. He buys 1,200 shares of a company he's never heard of before at a cost of $26.80 per share, paying the bargain commission rate on this transaction. What is the cost basis per share for this stock?

    _____

For each of the following scenarios, provide both the total cost and the cost basis per share figures.

5. 300 shares of stock at $55 each, with a commission paid of $125

    Total cost _____

    Cost basis per share _____

6. 10 shares of stock at $8.50 each, with a commission paid of $28

    Total cost _____

    Cost basis per share _____

Chapter 5: Stock Purchases and Cost Basis (cont.)

7. 500 shares of stock at $23.75 each, with a commission paid of $100

    Total cost _____

    Cost basis per share _____

8. 5,075 shares of stock at $30.50 per share, with a commission paid of $450

    Total cost _____

    Cost basis per share _____

9. 20,000 shares of stock at $1.10 per share; purchased in two different blocks of 10,000 shares; with a commission paid of $100 on each block

    Total cost _____

    Cost basis per share _____

10. 130 shares of stock at $98.50 per share, with a commission paid of $40

    Total cost _____

    Cost basis per share _____

11. Free commission offered by broker on a purchase of 100 shares at $34.40

    Total cost _____

    Cost basis per share _____

Questions to Consider

12. If you are buying a small number of shares of a relatively inexpensive stock (for example, 20 shares of a $10 stock), how does the commission affect the cost per share differently than buying a large number of shares of a more expensive company?

    _____

    _____

    _____

13. Why would the cost of commissions be of less worry to a person who only buys or sells stock a few times a year and selects only the stock of companies they plan to keep for a long time?

    _____

    _____

    _____

Chapter 6: Stock Dividend Policy

There are several different types of dividends. The basic types of cash dividends are:
- Regular cash dividends
- Extra cash dividends
- Special dividends
- Liquidating dividends

Other types of dividend options include:
- Stock dividends
- Stock split/reverse stock split
- Stock repurchase option

The most common type of dividend is a **cash dividend**. Typically, public companies pay regular cash dividends four times a year. As the name suggests, these are cash payments made directly to shareholders, and they are made in the regular course of business.

Sometimes, firms will pay regular cash dividends and an **extra cash dividend**. By calling part of the payment "extra," management is indicating that part of the dividend may or may not be repeated in the future.

A **special dividend** is similar, but as the name indicates, this dividend is viewed as truly unusual, or a one-time event that will probably never be repeated. This type of dividend is given when the company receives a very unexpected windfall, such as a major lawsuit settlement.

The payment of a **liquidating dividend** usually means that some or all of the business has been liquidated, or sold off. The money from the sale is distributed to the owners or shareholders in the form of dividends.

Another type of dividend is paid out in shares of stock. This type of dividend is called a **stock dividend**. A stock dividend is not really a true dividend, because it is not paid. The effect of a stock dividend is to increase the number of shares that each owner holds. Since there are more shares outstanding, each share is simply worth less.

A **stock split** is essentially the same thing as a stock dividend. When a stock split is declared, each share is split up to create additional shares. For example, in a three-for-one split, each old share is split into three new shares.

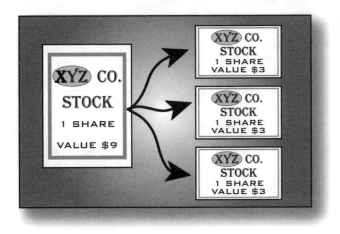

A less frequently used financial maneuver is a **reverse stock split**. In a one-for-three reverse split, each investor exchanges three old shares for one new share. The new share is now worth the same as the three old shares combined. The company's financial statements do not change, and the value of the investment does not change. The reasons why a firm would execute a reverse split are as follows: (1) in having fewer shares, the transaction costs of buying and selling will be less for investors; or (2) potential investors like to see the price of shares within a certain range.

17

Chapter 6: Stock Dividend Policy (cont.)

Some markets, like the NYSE, require a corporation's stock to be above a minimum price in order to be traded on their exchange.

An alternative to paying a cash dividend is the **stock repurchasing** option. Stock repurchasing has become a major financial option in recent years and will likely continue to be an alternative to cash dividends. There is literally no major effect on the company or the investor when the company chooses a stock purchase versus a cash dividend. The outflow of money is the same, whether the company gives dividends or repurchases an equivalent amount of stock from the marketplace. For shareholders, theoretically, the market value of their stock goes down equal to the amount of the cash dividend, thus having no effect on the investors' total worth.

Example:

If the XYZ Company is worth 1 million dollars and has 100,000 shares outstanding, then the stock value is $10 per share ($1,000,000 ÷ 100,000 shares = $10). If you have 100 shares of XYZ Corporation, and the stock is currently worth $10 per share, your worth in this company is $1,000 (100 shares x $10 = $1,000). Now, if the company decides to pay a $1 dividend ($1 x 100,000 shares), then the company will be worth $100,000 less, or $900,000 ($1,000,000 – $100,000). The value of each share is now worth $9 ($900,000 ÷ 100,000 shares = $9 each). Investors now have 100 shares worth $9 each (100 shares x $9 = $900) plus $100 in cash from dividends, for a total of $1,000.

If the company opted for a stock repurchase of $100,000, then the company would be worth $900,000, and they would buy back 10,000 shares, making the value of each share now $10 ($900,000 net worth ÷ 90,000 shares = $10 per share). Thus, if you owned 100 shares as an investor, your worth in this company is the same (100 shares x $10 = $1,000). The only difference to shareholders with a stock repurchase is that they don't have to pay the extra income tax. For the corporation, we can view the stock repurchase option as the company getting "leaner and meaner."

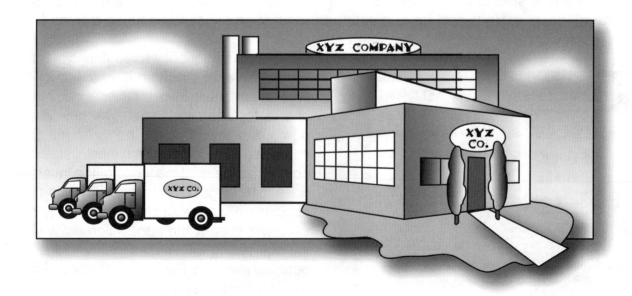

Chapter 7: Stock Splits

Companies use stock splits to adjust the price of a stock without really changing the true value of stockholders' holdings in the company. The majority of companies have stocks that trade in the $5 to $60 range. When the price of a stock rises over about $80, and especially when the price of a stock gets over $100, it begins to look pricey to investors who cannot afford to buy the stock in 100-block units. Stocks may be bought and sold in almost any quantity, but 100-share (and larger) blocks are something of a traditional benchmark for stock trades. Stock splits give a company a way to manage the share price when the price gets too high or too low, without affecting the stock's underlying value.

Here's how the typical stock split works. First, a company will announce the date they plan to do the stock split and the date on which you must own the stock to be eligible for the stock split. The typical stock split works on a simple ratio. A "2-for-1 split" is the most common, and it means that for every share of stock you own, you'll receive one new share of stock. Likewise a 3-for-1 split means that for every share of stock you own in the company, you'll end up with three after the split (the one share you had, plus the 2 new ones). An easy way to think of it is turning in your "old" shares of company stock and receiving the stated ratio back in "new" shares.

Once the new shares are issued in a stock split, almost like magic, the price of the stock adjusts on the market to reflect the split, since more shares of the company's stock now exist.

Stock splits can work in reverse as well in something called a "reverse split." This typically happens when a company's stock falls below $1. The company takes in many shares, returning fewer shares to the investor after the split. This is done in an effort to raise the per-share price. Reverse splits are generally seen as a sign of trouble, and many investors will bail out of a company's stock when a reverse split is announced.

Examples:
A. An investor owns 1,000 shares in a manufacturing company that has announced a 3-for-1 stock split. Once the split has taken place, how many shares of stock will the investor have?

In a 3-for-1 stock split, one share owned becomes three shares after the split. So 1,000 shares will become 3,000 shares after the split.

B. An investor owns 80 shares of stock in an entertainment company that has announced a 3-for-2 stock split. Once the split has taken place, how many shares of stock will the investor have?

In a 3-for-2 stock split, two shares owned become three shares after the split. So 80 shares will become 120 shares after the split.

C. Miranda owns 44 shares of stock in a company that sells discount carpet. They have announced a 2-for-1 stock split. How many shares will she own after the split has taken place?

In a 2-for-1 stock split, one share owned becomes two shares after the split. So 44 shares will become 88 after the split.

Name: _____ Date: _____

Chapter 7: Stock Splits (cont.)

Directions: For each situation described, find the number of shares held after the specified split has taken place. One question asks you to solve a stock split ratio.

1. The Fantastic Discoveries Mineral Rights and Patents Company has announced a 3-for-2 stock split. The CEO of the company owns 1,200,000 shares. How many shares will the CEO have after the split takes place?

   _____

2. The Oil, Electric, and Gas Profit Corporation of Western Oregon has announced a 3-for-1 stock split. Carmen owns 75 shares in this company. How many shares will she have after the split takes place?

   _____

3. Goliath Oak Tree Land Management and Timber Trust Company has suffered some set-backs in its business operations. Its company stock price has hovered at around $1 per share for several months. The company has 200,000 outstanding shares. After a 1-for-10 reverse split takes place, how many outstanding shares will there be in this company?

   _____

4. Reynard works for a fashion company with publicly traded stock. He heard a rumor at a fashion show that a competitor will be announcing a 3-for-1 stock split soon, and the stock price is expected to rise on that news. He does not want to be disloyal to his own company, but the stock split sounds too tempting to miss. If Reynard purchases 2,000 shares of the competitor's stock, how many shares will he have after the split?

   _____

5. Smith, Lemming, and Associates Asbestos Chemical Cleanup Corporation announced a 1-for-10,000 stock split, hoping to pull the share price up from the current price of 2 cents per share. The chairman of the company hopes to settle all pending lawsuits and to eventually move the company into less risky areas. Owning 50,000 shares of this company's stock, Owen hopes for a speedy recovery and a return to the company's paying of dividends again. How many shares will Owen have after the reverse split has taken place?

   _____

6. Jill has just received a notice, stating that her 60 shares of stock in the Glass, Fabric, and Faux Steel Design Decorating Company will become 240 shares after an announced stock split takes place. What is the ratio of this stock split?

   _____

Chapter 8: Dividend Payment

As was pointed out in Chapter 6, when dividends are paid, the value of the stock goes down proportionately to the amount of dividend. Similarly, just before dividends are paid, the stock may hold special value for those investors seeking cash dividends. Whether an investor is looking for cheaper stock, or cash dividends, usually depends on which income tax bracket they are in.

There is a legal procedure for the payment of dividends. This four-step procedure is described below.

- **Declaration date** – The board of directors declares a payment of dividends, and payment of said dividends becomes a legal liability to the corporation.

- **Ex-dividend date** – To make sure that the dividend checks go to the right people, brokerage firms and stock exchanges established an ex-dividend date. This date is two business days before the date of record (discussed next). If you buy on this date or after, then the previous stockowner will get the dividend.

- **Record date** – Based on its records, the corporation prepares a list of all the individuals believed to be stockholders. The word "believed" is important here. If you bought the stock shortly before this date, the corporation's records may not reflect that fact because of mailing or other delays. Without some modification, some of the dividend checks will get mailed to the wrong people. This is the reason for the ex-dividend date.

- **Date of payment** – This is the date the dividend checks are actually mailed.

MAY				1	2	3
4	5	6	7	8	9	10
11	12	13	14 Ex-Dividend	15	16 Record Date	17
18	19	20	21	22 Payment	23	24
25	26	27	28	29	30	31

Chapter 9: Dividend Yield

While banks pay interest on deposits, some companies also pay a form of interest to shareholders. Dividends are payments made to the owners of a company's stock as a bonus for those who own the shares. In this way, companies can attract investors who are hoping that the company's stock price will rise, but are satisfied to collect dividends while they wait.

Dividends are typically paid each quarter. Most stocks that pay dividends carry a quarterly dividend payment of under $1, with the majority being in the 10-cent to 50-cent range. These dividends may not sound very substantial, but it can be a good incentive for investors to buy a company's shares and hold them for the income that dividends produce. If you have a lot of shares in a company that pays a good dividend, there can be substantial income produced by the dividend payments. Many investors won't even consider buying the stock of a company that doesn't pay dividends.

Figuring the dividend yield is a basic piece of information that is essential for the investor interested in dividends. The **yield** is a percentage figure that represents what the dividend pays back in relation to the price of the stock. The dividend yield provides a handy figure for comparing the stock to other investments.

The formula for finding the dividend yield of a stock is very simple:

Dividend ÷ Stock Price = Yield

Examples:
  A. A shipping company's stock costs $100 per share and pays a yearly dividend of $2. What is this company's dividend yield?

$2 ÷ $100 = yield, so $0.02 = Yield (The yield is 2%.)

  B. An investor is considering a manufacturing company's stock that closed the day at $24 per share. This company pays a quarterly dividend of 40 cents. What is the dividend yield of this stock?

$0.40 ÷ $24 = 0.0167 (quarterly yield),
so $.0167 x 4 = 0.0668 (annual yield) The annual yield is 6.68%.

Directions: For each of the situations, compute the dividend yield.

1. Stock is at $20 per share, and pays a yearly dividend of $1.

    _____

2. Stock is at $60 per share, and pays a yearly dividend of $1.80.

    _____

3. Stock is at $32.20 per share, and pays a yearly dividend of $1.20.

    _____

4. Stock is at $8 per share, and pays a quarterly dividend of $0.25.

    _____

Name: _____ Date: _____

Chapter 9: Dividend Yield (cont.)

5. Stock is at $2.50 per share, and pays a yearly dividend of $0.10.

   _____

6. Stock is at $42 per share, and pays a yearly dividend of $2.80.

   _____

7. Stock is at $122 per share, and pays a yearly dividend of $1.04.

   _____

8. Stock is at $62.60 per share, and pays a quarterly dividend of $1.80.

   _____

9. Stock is at $38.40 per share, and pays a quarterly dividend of $0.28.

   _____

10. The XZ & YJ Music Entertainment Film Company has just raised its yearly dividend to $1.10. Investors didn't seem to notice the change, as the stock price has remained at a steady $12. What is the dividend yield on this stock?

    _____

11. An investor has been monitoring the stock price of a company that manufactures machine parts and farm equipment. The company pays a quarterly dividend of $0.22. The stock price is currently $18.40. The investor has noticed that the stock price has recently dipped as low as $17.60. The investor thinks the stock will drop back to the $17.60 range again, if he is just patient. What is the difference in dividend yield if this investor waits to buy the stock at $17.60, instead of paying $18.40?

    _____

12. Mary wants to use $35,000 to buy an expensive piano. Through research, Mary has learned that this particular piano brand tends to appreciate in value at an average of 3.2% per year. Mary is thinking of the piano as an investment that can also be enjoyed. Mary's father has advised her to put her money into a stock that pays a $1.40 yearly dividend. The stock's price is currently at $26.60. Mary would like to examine each investment in an analytical way before making a final decision. How much better is the yield per year on the stock than on the piano?

    _____

Chapter 10: How to Read a Stock Table

If you check the *Wall Street Journal* or other newspapers for stock information, you will find information on a large number of stocks in several different markets. A sample of listings on the stock page from a *Wall Street Journal* is shown on the next page.

Once you are the proud owner of stocks, you will want to keep track of them. The easiest way to track your stock is through the daily newspapers or journals. First, you need to know under which exchange your stock is listed; i.e., NYSE, AMEX, or NASDAQ. Let's look at the tables column-by-column from left to right.

The first column, **YTD % CHG**, stands for **year-to-date percent of change**, which means that from a year ago to today, the stock price has changed by this percent.

The next two columns, **52 WEEK HI/LO**, give the stock's **high and low selling price peak** over the past year.

The next column, **STOCK (SYM)**, gives the name or an abbreviated version of the **stock's name** and the **stock symbol** used on the exchange.

The next column, **DIV**, is the **annual cash dividend** based upon the rate of the last quarterly dividend.

The next column, **YLD %**, provides the **yield percentages**, calculated by dividing the cash dividend by the closing price of the stock.

The next column, **PE**, is the **P/E ratio**; this figure gives the closing price divided by the annual earnings, based on the last four quarters.

The next column, **VOL 100s**, represents the **number of shares that were traded that day**, represented in hundreds. Thus, if the Vol 100s number is 1219, this means that 121,900 shares of this stock were traded.

The next column, **CLOSE**, represents the **price the stock closed that day**.

The last column, **NET CHG**, indicates the **point change** (either up or down) **from today's opening price**.

It is vitally important that investors familiarize themselves with the "How to Read This Table" section of the *Wall Street Journal*. This index is usually shown at the beginning of the NYSE Composite Transactions section. As you scan the stock tables, you will notice many symbols listed. All of the symbols are explained in the "How to Read this Table" section, and this valuable information should not be overlooked.

Chapter 10: How to Read a Stock Table (cont.)

Sample listings in the *Wall Street Journal*

THE WALL STREET JOURNAL.   FRIDAY, OCTOBER 4, 2002 **C3**

NEW YORK STOCK EXCHANGE COMPOSITE TRANSACTIONS

A

YTD %CHG	52-WEEK HI	LO	STOCK (SYM)	DIV	YLD %	PE	VOL 100s	CLOSE	NET CHG
-47.7	14	4.15	AAR **AIR**	.10	2.1	dd	600	4.71	-0.20
-11.6	19.75	12.63	ABM Ind **ABM s**	.36	2.6	21	1219	13.85	-0.05
-61.1	39.21	8.70	AOL Time **AOL**		…	dd	180022	12.49	0.17
-37.2	**19.99**	**8.20**	**AT&T T**	**.15**	**1.3**	**…**	**191200**	**11.40**	**-0.66**
-24.0	58	29.80	AbbottLab **ABT**	.94	2.2	25	44722	42.39	0.74
-36.6	**36.65**	**16.60**	**Abercrombie A ANF**	**…**		**10**	**23915**	**16.81**	**-1.32**
▼ **-81.9**	**50.80**	**11.06**	**AllmericaFNnl AFC.25**		**3.1**	**dd**	**33452**	**8.08**	**-3.43**
8.2	57.90	41.58	Aus&NZ Bk **ANZ**	2.06e	4.2	…	15	49.45	0.75

B

YTD %CHG	52-WEEK HI	LO	STOCK (SYM)	DIV	YLD %	PE	VOL 100s	CLOSE	NET CHG
-7.5	46.85	32.72	BASF ADS **BF**	1.14e	3.2	…	1581	35.06	0.24
▼ **-63.2**	**24.10**	**8.77**	**BallyTtlFit BFT**		**…**	**3**	**23280**	**7.93**	**-0.92**
-8.9	42.88	28.92	BkOne **ONE**	.84	2.4	14	67054	35.56	-1.55
▲ 22.4	30.62	23.25	BayVwCapl		…	…	616	30.67	0.07
-57.2	53.75	18.50	BestBuy **BYY s**		…	12	35445	21.26	0.08
-11.5	51.07	31.58	Boeing **BA**	.68	2.0	13	36509	34.31	-0.07
162.2	19.20	4.01	BoydGaming **BYD**		…	25	8757	17.04	-0.46
-40.2	**45.30**	**20.85**	**BrasilTel ADS BRP**	**1.42e**	**5.7**	**…**	**1134**	**24.81**	**1.31**

C

YTD %CHG	52-WEEK HI	LO	STOCK (SYM)	DIV	YLD %	PE	VOL 100s	CLOSE	NET CHG
-8.0	43.50	25.51	CACI Int A **CAI s**		…	31	2790	36.31	-0.18
-25.2	111	69.20	CIGNA **CI**	1.32	1.9	11	9046	69.30	-2.45
-71.1	**19.56**	**4.30**	**CTS Cp CPY**	**.12**	**2.6**	**dd**	**982**	**4.59**	**-0.31**
-28.2	59.99	36.33	Caterpillar **CAT**	1.40	3.7	20	14217	37.49	-0.29
39.5	7.10	3.25	CenterTr **CTA**	.24	4.0	22	661	5.93	0.03

Chapter 11: Stock Market Averages and Indexes

One of the popular ways to keep track of movement in the stock market is to turn on the television and check the Dow or one of the other familiar indexes. More precisely, the Dow is the DJIA, which stands for the **Dow Jones Industrial Average**. These numbers are widely publicized, but it is surprising how many people do not understand what they actually mean, although most of us have come to realize that up is good news, and down is bad news.

The Dow Jones Industrial Average (DJIA) is the most widely followed stock market average. When people talk about the stock market in general, they almost always refer to what the DJIA was doing lately. Charles Dow originally calculated the DJIA in 1884. This first average consisted of 11 major stocks. The prices of these 11 stocks were simply added together and divided by 11, yielding the DJIA. In 1928, the number of stocks in the DJIA was increased to 30. The divisor has been adjusted over the years (no longer equal to the number of stocks in the average) to take into consideration the many variables that affect the value of different stocks, such as price, number of shares outstanding, stock splits, and dividend policies.

Standard & Poor's Corporation has six different indices. The **S & P 500 Stock Index** is also called the **Composite Index**. The original S & P was comprised of 233 different stocks, but in 1957, it was increased to 500, to better reflect the entire market.

The **American Stock Exchange (AMEX) Market Value Index** measures the performance of 800 stocks listed on the AMEX. The AMEX Index was first introduced in 1973.

The **NASDAQ Indices** have become widely followed recently because of the increasing interest in high-technology stocks. The NASDAQ Composite Index measures the performance of 6,000 stocks listed on the NASDAQ exchange.

The **Wilshire 5000 Equity Index** was first introduced in 1974. This index, with 7,200 stocks, is the broadest index and the most representative of the movements in the overall market.

Chapter 12: The New York Stock Exchange

Stocks are traded on a variety of stock exchanges in the United States. The largest and most familiar exchange in the world is the **New York Stock Exchange (NYSE)**. This exchange lists over 3,000 individual companies, with stock values worth over 10 trillion dollars, and handles over 250 billion shares of stock. These are staggering numbers, especially when we typically track the market or DJIA and see a movement of a few points a day, one way or the other. It is hard to imagine the total dynamics of the NYSE market. In the 1950s, the number of traded shares averaged approximately 3 million per day. In the 1960s, the average number of shares traded daily rose to approximately 15 million. By the 1970s, the number of shares traded daily doubled, to approximately 30 million. The number of traded shares exploded during the 1980s to 100 million traded on any given day. The number of shares traded on the NYSE has continued to grow to over 500 million in the 1990s, and 900 million has been a common number of shares traded per day recently.

The origins of the NYSE date back to 1817. The founders set the rules and procedures for trading on the NYSE. Originally, the president of the NYSE Exchange Board read a list of available stocks twice a day, and members shouted buy and sell orders from their assigned chairs at the NYSE. Now we know where the phrase "having a seat on the NYSE" comes from. Today, the NYSE has about 1,400 exchange members, who are said to own "seats" on the exchange. Collectively, the members of the exchange are its owners. Exchange seat owners can buy and sell securities on the exchange floor without paying commissions. For this and other reasons, exchange seats are valuable assets and are bought and sold regularly. In recent years, exchange seats have sold for over 20 million dollars.

The largest number of NYSE members are registered as "commission brokers." About 500 NYSE members are commission brokers. Their primary responsibility is to get the best possible price for their orders. Commission brokers are typically employees of brokerage companies like Merrill Lynch.

The second-largest group of NYSE members are called "specialists." They are called specialists because they each focus on a small set of securities. Specialists are also referred to as "market makers," because they are obligated to maintain a fair, orderly market for the securities assigned to them. The specialists "make a market" by standing ready to buy at bid prices and sell at the asked prices, when there is a temporary disparity between the flow of buy orders and sell orders for their assigned securities.

The third-largest group of exchange members are called "floor brokers." Commission brokers who are too busy to handle certain orders themselves use floor brokers. Such commission brokers will assign some orders to floor brokers for execution (buy or sell). Floor brokers are sometimes referred to as "$2 brokers," a name earned at a time when the standard fee for their services was only $2.

In order to be listed on the NYSE, firms must meet certain minimum criteria. For example, a company is expected to have a market value for its publicly held shares of at least 18 million dollars, and a total of at least 2,000 shareholders, holding at least 100 shares each. There are additional minimum criteria on earnings, assets, and number of shares outstanding.

The American Stock Exchange (AMEX) lists the stock of smaller and newer companies than those listed on the NYSE. The companies listed on the AMEX are considered to be emerging growth companies; that is, companies that are not quite seasoned enough to be listed on the NYSE, which mostly lists older, more established companies.

Chapter 13: The NASDAQ Market

In terms of the number of companies listed and, on many days, the number of shares traded, the NASDAQ is even bigger than the NYSE. The market's somewhat odd name comes from the acronym **NASDAQ**, which stands for **National Association of Security Dealers Automated Quotations system**.

Introduced in 1971, the NASDAQ market is a computer network of securities dealers who release timely security price quotes to NASDAQ subscribers. These dealers act as market makers for securities listed on the NASDAQ. As market makers, NASDAQ dealers post bid and asked prices, at which they accept sell and buy orders, respectively. With each price quote, they also post the number of stock shares that they obligate themselves to trade at their quoted prices.

Unlike the NYSE specialist system, NASDAQ requires that there be multiple market makers for actively traded stocks. Thus, there are two key differences between the NYSE and NASDAQ: (1) NASDAQ is a computer network and has no physical location where trading takes place, and (2) NASDAQ has a multiple market maker system, rather than a specialist system. All the trading done through the NASDAQ is through dealers.

There are about 5,500 securities that are listed on the NASDAQ system, with an average of about a dozen market makers for each security. Traditionally, shares of stock in smaller companies were listed on the NASDAQ, and there was a tendency for companies to move from the NASDAQ to the NYSE, once they became large enough. Today, however, giant companies such as Microsoft, MCI, and Intel have chosen to remain on the NASDAQ.

The NASDAQ network operates with three different levels of information access. **Level 1 terminals** are designed to provide registered representatives with a timely, accurate source of price quotations for their clients. **Level 2 terminals** connect market makers with brokers and other dealers and allow subscribers to view price quotes from all NASDAQ market makers. **Level 3 terminals** are for the use of market makers only. These terminals allow NASDAQ dealers to enter or change their price quote information.

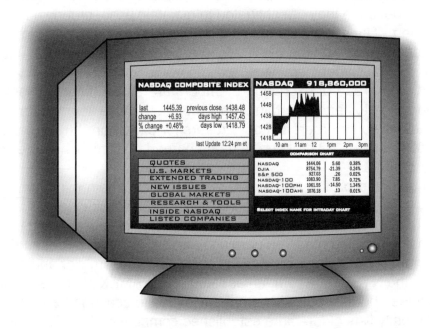

Chapter 14: Basic Stock Analysis

There are literally hundreds of variables that one can analyze when evaluating individual stocks. There is a possibility that by the time you collect all the necessary data, analyze it, interpret it, and make a buy decision, you'll buy too late to get the price you want. As we all know, the way to make money in the stock market is to buy low and sell high. With this in mind, let's discuss some basics; we can always get more sophisticated as time goes on.

It is important to note that individual investors have a major advantage over professional and institutional investors for several reasons. Professional and institutional investors spend a lot of time analyzing possible investments, thus entering the market late, basically following the herd. In the same vein, a stock does not become attractive to brokerage houses until large institutional investors recognize the possible opportunities. As a result, professional investors jump on the bandwagon after the stock has already been run up in price by these large institutional fund managers.

As people are trying to make a living and being tuned in to "what's hot and what's not" in the marketplace, with our families and friends, we are literally years ahead of the big-time analyzers. As investors, if we know nothing else, we should only invest in companies with products and/or services that we know are quality product offerings, at a value. If we truly believe in and use the product, then chances are the company will be successful. We should buy and hold the stock as long as we truly believe in the company's product offering. The first rule of investing is to understand and believe in the company and its products in which you are investing. Some obvious examples today would be McDonald's and Wal-Mart.

Chapter 14: Basic Stock Analysis (cont.)

Besides our own visceral (gut) feelings, there are two other variables, at a minimum, that we need to analyze. These two important variables are **earnings per share (EPS)** and **price-to-earnings ratio (P/E ratio)**.

The earnings per share (EPS) ratio is one of the most widely used measures of a stock's valuation. At face value, the EPS ratio is a good measure of the stock, but if you are unaware of its limitations, it can be greatly misleading. First, let's look at the basic formula for computing Earnings Per Share.

Formula: Net Income ÷ Total Shares Outstanding = EPS (earnings per share)

The higher the EPS, the better; thus, it might be a good tool to use when evaluating a company. One thing we need to take notice of is whether the company also has preferred stock. If so, dividends payable to preferred stock need to be deducted from net income before calculating the EPS. There are other variables you will want to check out before relying on EPS in your investment decisions. Some companies have convertible securities, like stock options and warrants. **Convertible securities** means that there is a potential for the number of common stock shares outstanding to increase when these options are activated, thus having a negative effect on EPS.

In conclusion, most investors view EPS as an important tool in evaluating stocks. Because of the popularity of this ratio, most financial papers and journals report the EPS daily. Furthermore, corporations are required to report the EPS of their stocks in quarterly and annual reports.

Another widely used tool for assessing stocks is the price-to-earnings ratio (P/E ratio). A high P/E ratio suggests that the market expects good earnings growth. A low P/E ratio would indicate that the market expects earnings growth to be sluggish. Let's look at the formula for calculating a firm's P/E ratio.

Formula: P/E ratio = Price per share ÷ EPS (which is calculated above)

The P/E ratios of all stocks are reported daily in the popular financial papers and journals. As said earlier, a high P/E ratio is typically viewed as good. However, if the firm had little or no net income, and because of the way the P/E ratio is calculated, the P/E ratio would be artificially high and, in this case, would be bad. So, once again, investors beware—if it looks too good to be true, then it probably is. One way to verify whether a stock's P/E ratio is abnormally high or low is to check a reliable source like the *Wall Street Journal*, *Barron's*, or *Investor's Business Daily*.

Name: _____   Date: _____

Chapter 15: Price-to-Earnings Ratio

A company's net earnings are important, of course, since the figure represents how much money a company is making. A company can borrow money when times are lean or if the business needs to expand, but over a sustained period of time, the company must have earnings in order to remain a viable business. As such, earnings represent one of the main numbers to which an investor might pay attention, when analyzing a company's stock.

One tool for looking at earnings is a company's P/E ratio (price-to-earnings ratio). Simply, this P/E figure answers the question: How expensive is this stock in regard to what this company earns? Here's how P/E works:

Per Share Price of Stock ÷ Earnings per Share (EPS) = P/E ratio (price-to-earnings ratio)

The P/E ratio is important to investors, because the higher the number, the more expensive the stock is in terms of earnings. Most healthy companies whose stock is in good demand by investors will have P/E ratios in the range of perhaps 8 to 22. While there are no hard and fast boundaries, the P/E ratio is one of several factors investors use to gauge a stock's underlying value.

Example:

The Bunker Hill Shipwrecks and Salvage Claims Corporation had earnings of $1.88 in the previous year and expects the same for the coming year. The price of this stock is $30 per share. What is this company's P/E ratio?

$30 ÷ $1.88 = P/E ratio, so 15.96 = P/E ratio

Directions: Determine the P/E ratio in each of the following situations.

1. Stock price is $40 with earnings of $2.40. _____

2. Stock price is $22.10 with earnings of $2.80. _____

3. Stock price is $7.50 with earnings of $0.20. _____

4. Stock price is $190 with earnings of $8.25. _____

5. Stock price is $3.15 with earnings of $1.05. _____

6. Stock price is $88.50 with earnings of $3.65. _____

7. Stock price is $1.40 with earnings of $0.20. _____

Name: _____ Date: _____

Chapter 15: Price-to-Earnings Ratio (cont.)

Questions to Consider

8. If you're an investor interested in buying only companies with high-yield dividends, then why would P/E ratio mean anything to you?

    _____

    _____

    _____

9. Can you think of some reasons why a company with a reasonable P/E ratio still might not be a good investment?

    _____

    _____

    _____

10. Sometimes a company's stock price will decline on news that earnings will be less than expected. Why do you think this is the case?

    _____

    _____

    _____

11. In what scenario could a company's earnings rise sharply, but the company's dividend yield drop dramatically?

    _____

    _____

    _____

Name: _____ Date: _____

Chapter 16: Another Look at Cost Basis

Directions: Answer the following questions concerning total cost and cost basis per share.

1. Jennifer bought 220 shares of a shoe retailer's stock after visiting the store and hearing favorable reports from the sales staff working there. She paid $34.75 per share for this stock, and also paid a commission of $60 on the purchase. What is her total cost for this stock?

   _____

2. Alan watched as the price declined on a stock he'd been following. He put in an online order and managed to get 110 shares at $4.25. He always pays $18 for trades made online through his broker. What is his cost basis per share for this stock purchase?

   _____

3. James was called by his broker who suggested he purchase 1,000 shares of a new company at $22. James agreed to buy only 200 shares, in spite of his broker's persuasive arguments in favor of the new stock. Commission for this purchase was $85. What is James's total cost for this block of stock?

   _____

4. Beth bought 200 shares of stock in a restaurant chain at $18 per share. After eating at one of the locations, she decided to buy another 100 shares, but the price was a bit higher for this lot, $21 per share. She paid a commission each time of $35. What is her cost basis per share for the entire block of stock?

   _____

5. A fire was reported on a financial news channel as having wiped out the manufacturing facility of a company that makes fine glassware. Elizabeth, one of the firefighters who had fought the blaze, realized that the press had been mistaken; the blaze was only in an adjacent warehouse. So, Elizabeth called her broker and bought 1,200 shares of the glassware stock at a price of $10.25, even though her broker tried to talk her out of making the purchase. She paid a commission of $145 on this purchase. The next day, the stock surged back to $16.70 after it was correctly reported that the fire had not damaged this company's manufacturing facility. What is Elizabeth's cost basis per share for this stock?

   _____

6. Carol was given 3 shares of stock as a gift by her grandfather. Each share is worth $140. Carol paid a broker $25 commission to register the shares in her name and add them to her brokerage account. What was her total cost basis for the shares?

   _____

Name: _____ Date: _____

Chapter 17: Dollar Cost Averaging

Many investors buy the stock of a particular company on a regular basis in order to meet an investment goal. Sometimes, monies are invested weekly or monthly as it becomes available. This strategy allows the investor to accumulate a particular stock over a period of time.

Dollar cost averaging is a technique used for computing the cost of stock purchased over a period of time, in different blocks. Since the price of a stock tends to fluctuate from day to day, blocks of stock purchased at different times are likely to be bought at different price levels. Dollar cost averaging provides an accounting tool for investors to gauge their overall cost in a stock that has been purchased in different blocks at different prices.

Many investors use the figure obtained through dollar cost averaging to make decisions about when to sell a stock or whether to buy more shares of a particular stock. "Averaging down" is a term sometimes used by investors to note a quality stock whose price has moved lower, with additional shares of this stock having been bought at the lower price levels to supplement their position in the stock.

Beginning to sound complicated? The formula is actually simpler that the concept itself. Here's how dollar cost averaging works: take the total cost of all shares and divide by the total number of shares held. This yields the average price paid per share for the entire pool of stock. That's dollar cost averaging.

Example:

Breanne bought 12 shares of a company's stock, with a cost basis of $48, including commission. Later, she added 24 more shares of this stock to her portfolio, paying $108 for this block including commission. Use dollar cost averaging to find the average share price.

Formula: Total Cost ÷ Total Number of Shares = Average Price Per Share

($108 + $48) ÷ (12 + 24) = $4.33 (average price per share)

Directions: For each of the situations listed, use dollar cost averaging to determine the average price per share.

1. Maria bought 50 shares of a company's stock for $5,540, including commission. She later picked up another 50 shares for $4,880, including commission.

    _____

2. Ethan bought 20 shares of stock in a company that manages golf courses, paying $210 for the stock, including commission. He later added 30 more shares of this company's stock at a cost of $388, including commission.

    _____

Chapter 17: Dollar Cost Averaging (cont.)

3. Miguel bought the following blocks of stock in a company, paying the following amounts for each block, including commission:

    220 shares, cost $23,110   100 shares, cost $12,200

    50 shares, cost $6,800   500 shares, cost $55,000

    _____

4. Cynthia bought 100 shares of stock in a financial company at $44.50 per share, paying a commission of $22 on the purchase. She later bought 50 more shares at $38.75 and again paid a commission of $22 on the purchase.

    _____

5. Each month for one year, Howard bought 10-share blocks of stock in his favorite food company. Each time, he paid a commission of $16 to his online brokerage. The prices paid for each block of shares were as follows: $102, $110, $112.50, $116, $108, $98.50, $88, $92.25, $95, $98.75, $100, $102.

    _____

Questions to Consider

6. If the point of investing is to make as large a profit as possible, why use dollar cost averaging to buy stocks over a period of time? Wouldn't it be wiser to wait and buy the stock at its lowest point?

    _____

    _____

    _____

    _____

7. What is the major drawback of dollar cost averaging, and why does it present a problem?

    _____

    _____

    _____

    _____

Name: _____ Date: _____

Chapter 17: Another Look at Dollar Cost Averaging

Directions: For each of the situations listed, use dollar cost averaging to determine the average price per share.

1. Kevin bought 1,000 shares of a company's stock for $2,480, including commission. He later added another 200 shares of this same stock to his portfolio at a cost of $660.

   _____

2. Latasha bought 31 shares of a company's stock at $45.40 per share, paying a commission of $24 on the purchase. She later added another 29 shares of this stock to her holdings at $41.20 per share, paying a commission of $24 on the purchase.

   _____

3. A mutual fund manager made the following stock purchases in a media company, with the total cost for each transaction listed.
   11,000 shares, $242,800
   6,000 shares, $123,000
   2,000 shares, $53,200
   40,000 shares, $1,160,000

   _____

4. Juan bought 1,020 shares in a real estate management company at a price of $26.25 per share, paying a commission of $40 on the purchase. Because of a news report about a questionable deal made by the company, the stock price dropped. So, Juan was able to buy another 640 shares at a price of $20.75 per share, paying a commission of $40 on the purchase.

   _____

Questions to Consider

5. Describe how an investor can make money using dollar cost averaging, even if he or she ends up selling some shares at less than was paid for those shares.

   _____

   _____

   _____

6. Why would dollar cost averaging make little sense in the case of a company whose stock has been steadily declining, with little hope of a reasonable rebound in price?

   _____

   _____

   _____

Name: _____ Date: _____

Chapter 18: Stock Sales

    Investors sell stocks for a variety of reasons. Many investors will sell a stock once it has reached a predetermined price point, in order to realize a profit. For instance, if a stock's price has grown to a certain level, the investor may decide it is time to sell that stock, regardless of how well the company is actually doing. Some sell decisions are based on other reasons. If a company has setbacks or fails in its business plan, the price of the stock may decline. Many investors will sell stocks at the first hint of trouble in order to preserve their investment dollars, even if it means losing part of their initial investment.

    Selling stock is about as easy as buying it. People place sell orders by calling their broker or by sending the order online via computer. When a block of stock sells, the amount of money from the sale (called **total proceeds**) is transferred to the investor who sold the stock. Before this money is placed in the investor's account, commission for selling the stock is ordinarily deducted by the broker. **Profit** is any amount earned over and above the total cost of the stock, including all commissions. If total proceeds after commissions is less money than was first invested, then a **loss** has occurred.

Example:

    Shawn bought 300 shares of stock at $20 per share, paying a commission of $29 on the purchase. When the stock was sold, the shares brought $23 each, and the commission paid on the sale was $29. What was Shawn's profit on this stock?

Sold 300 shares at $23 per share, total proceeds = $6,900

Total commissions charged, 2 x $29	- $ 58
Cost of stock: 300 shares at $20 per share	- $6,000
Profit	$ 842

    If the number in our profit row had been negative, then it would represent a loss on this investment. Losses can be denoted with a pair of brackets. **Example:** < 200 >

Directions: For each of the following situations, determine the profit < or loss > in the following stock transactions.

1. Gordon bought 700 shares of an oil company's stock for $15.60 per share. He paid a commission of $80 on this purchase. When the stock was sold only a short time later, the shares brought $16.40 each, and he again paid an $80 commission on the sale.

    _____

2. Jane paid a commission of $35 to sell 200 shares of stock she'd bought in an agricultural products manufacturer. The shares sold at $17.70 each. When she bought the stock, it was only $8 per share. At the time of purchase, she paid a $22 commission.

    _____

Chapter 18: Stock Sales (cont.)

3. Timothy bought 525 shares of a company's stock at $25 per share, paying a commission of $65 on the purchase. Only a short time later, he noticed a better deal and needed to free up some money by selling the 525 shares. Timothy paid another $65 commission on the sale, and the shares had dropped to $24.75 per share by the time they were sold.

   _____

4. Russell spent $10,200 to buy 1,000 shares of stock in a company. Four years later, he sold 700 of these shares at $28 per share, paying a $40 commission on the sale. Only a month after that, he sold the last 300 shares of this stock for $26.50 per share, once again paying a $40 commission.

   _____

5. Roscoe jumps in and out of stocks, trying to make fast profits. He does all of his trades online and pays a flat rate commission of $12 per transaction. In the afternoon, he sold 75 shares of a company at $22.10. He'd bought that stock just that morning, paying $21.80 per share.

   _____

6. Tony was given 1,200 shares of stock in a company after his grandfather's estate was settled. His broker processed the transfer of these shares into Tony's brokerage account free of charge. Tony decided to sell this stock, placing one order per month to sell 100 shares until all shares were sold within a one-year time frame. Tony's broker charged a commission of $75 for each of these sell transactions. The per-share prices received for the blocks of stock each month were as follows: $55, $54, $54.40, $48.50, $49.75, $51, $49, $44.80, $41, $40.40, $38, $40.25.

   _____

7. Charlotte was shocked to see that a company whose stock she'd paid $30.80 per share for had dropped to $21 in response to some bad news. She decided to sell the shares, and the 90 shares of stock brought $19.75 each by the time she could get her broker on the phone to place a sell order. Commission both ways was $38.

   _____

Name: _____ Date: _____

Chapter 18: Another Look at Stock Sales

Directions: For each of the following situations, determine the profit < or loss > in the following stock transactions.

1. Will sold a block of 200 shares of stock he'd been holding for many years. The stock sold for $48 per share, and he paid a commission of $35 on the sale. When he'd originally bought the stock, he only paid $8.25 per share and a commission of $12 on the purchase.

    _____

2. Georgina paid $905, including the commission, for 140 shares of stock in a book publishing company. She paid a commission of $18 to sell this stock, and $1,215.75 was deposited into her brokerage account after the trade had settled.

    _____

3. Benjamin bought 250 shares of stock in a high tech company at $27.75 per share, paying a commission of $28 on the purchase. Soon after, he realized he'd done little research about this company and did not understand its products. Benjamin sold all of the shares at $27.25, once again paying $28 commission.

    _____

4. Sandra bought 100 shares of a company's stock for $38 per share. She managed to sell the 100 shares for $4.25 more per share than she'd paid. Her online commission to buy or sell a stock is always $16.95 per trade.

    _____

5. Eric bought 300 shares of stock in a paper manufacturing company, paying a bargain price of $6 per share and a commission of $24. A month later, he bought another 200 shares, but the stock price had risen to $7.50. Commission for this purchase was also $24. Later, he sold his entire block of stock in the paper company at $12 per share, once again paying his regular $24 commission on the sale.

    _____

6. A group of investors pooled their money to buy the 10,000 outstanding shares in a small mining company. There were no commissions paid on this transfer; it was done directly with the owners of the stock. The investors paid their own lawyer $1,500 to arrange the stock transfer. The price paid for the stock was $185,000. The group of investors later sold the stock for $220,000. Once again, their lawyer was paid to handle the legal papers, this time at a cost of $2,000.

    _____

Section III: Bond Issues

Chapter 19: Bonds

Purchasing bonds is a much safer investment than purchasing common stock, but the investor is limited in the amount of return on the investment. Simply stated, a **bond** is an IOU, issued by one of three kinds of institutions. The three sets of institutions are: corporations, the United States government and its agencies, and/or states, towns, or municipalities. Usually, corporations issue bonds for large capital investments, such as new buildings and factories. The U.S. government might issue bonds to help pay for wartime expenses. States and towns might issue bonds to pay for highway and bridge construction.

When you purchase a bond, you are basically lending money to one of the three sets of institutions. In return for lending the money, the institution pays the investor a preset interest amount (usually semiannually). At the end of the bond contract, the institution makes its last interest payment, and also pays back the amount originally borrowed.

Now that we have a basic understanding of how bonds work, let's attach the market jargon to our discussion. The bond's purchase price is referred to as the bond's **face value**. If it is a brand-new bond issue, the face value is $1,000. If it is an issue that has been around for a while, then the price might be higher or lower than $1,000, depending on today's interest rates. For example, if a bond was originally issued at 6% (which is referred to as the **coupon rate**), and today's interest rate is only 4%, then you would be willing to pay more (a **premium**) for the bond, because the old bond issue will yield more than a new bond with a 4% coupon rate would. Conversely, if today's interest rate is 8%, then you would want to pay face value, because you could earn more on a new bond issue. Paying less than face value is referred to as paying a **discount**. You will notice when looking up different bond values in the newspaper that they are reported in hundreds, rather than thousands. So, if a bond is listed at 103, then it is selling at a premium at $1,030.

The issuer of the bond is legally obligated to pay back the face value of the bond on a set date; this is referred to as the **maturity date**. Bonds fall into one of two time-related categories. If the maturity date is less than ten years, then it is referred to as a **short-term**, or **intermediate bond**. If the maturity date is ten or more years, then it is referred to as a **long-term bond**.

Another type of bond in the marketplace is the **zero coupon bond**. A zero coupon bond does not make semiannual interest payments, but instead calculates the value of all of the coupon payments at a compounded rate until maturity, and then subtracts this amount from the face value to determine the selling price. This is similar to the familiar U.S. Savings Bond. You can go to a bank or post office and buy a U.S. Savings Bond for around $80, and, at a predetermined date in the future, you can cash in the bond for $100. The advantage to the issuer is that they do not have to pay or be concerned with the semiannual interest payments. This is also a good way for investors to save a certain amount of money for a future purchase (a down payment for a house, college education, a big-screen TV, etc.).

Chapter 20: How to Evaluate Bonds

Bond issuers are legally obligated to pay the semiannual coupon rate and the bond's face value at the date of maturity. Sometimes, because of financial difficulties, the bond issuer will make late payments or no payments at all, which is referred to as a **default**. There are two leading independent companies that track bond issuers and their payment records. These two independent rating services are Moody's and Standard & Poor's; their publications are available at most libraries. Moody's and Standard & Poor's rating systems are listed below.

BOND RATINGS

Moody's		Standard & Poor's
Aaa	Top Quality	AAA
Aa	Excellent	AA
A	Very High	A
Baa	Medium	BBB
Ba	Speculative	BB
B	Lower Speculative	B
Caa	Poor and Risky	CCC
Ca	Near Default	CC
C	Default	C

Companies with the highest ratings will pay the lowest coupon rates, because they are the safest. Companies with lower ratings will have to pay slightly higher coupon rates to entice the more speculative investor.

Name: _____ Date: _____

Chapter 21: Bond Yields

We know that bonds are essentially loans made by investors to companies and also to local or federal governments. Bonds pay interest and produce a yield, just as dividend-paying stocks do. In this activity, we'll concentrate on bond yields, since this aspect of bond trading is fairly straightforward.

Bonds are also like stocks, in that sometimes they trade at different price levels, depending on the underlying circumstances of the bond, such as the interest rate offered (coupon) or the creditworthiness of the company involved. A bond originally issued at $1,000 face value, and paying 5% interest, may actually trade for substantially less than $1,000 if there is concern about the company's ability to pay back the bond with the interest due at maturity. If this particular bond issue drops in price (discounts) to $800, then the yield of 5% has changed as well. For this reason, bond trading represents a fairly specialized field, perhaps even more so than buying and selling stocks.

The general formula for bond yields:

Coupon ÷ Price = Yield

Example: A particular company bond was offered at $1,000 with a coupon of 4%. After a time, the bond is discounted to $960 to stimulate sales of this bond. What is the current yield? (Keep in mind that in bond terminology, this bond will be listed at 96.)

4% ÷ 96 = Yield, so 4.17% is the new yield.

Directions: Determine the bond yield in each of the following situations.

1. Coupon is 3.5%, bond is at a premium at $1,020. _____

2. Coupon is 10.5%, bond is at a discount at $860. _____

3. Coupon is at 14.75%, bond is at face value of $1,000. _____

4. Coupon is at 8.8%, bond is at a discount at $980. _____

5. Coupon is at 12.2%, bond is at a premium at $1,050. _____

Name: _____ Date: _____

Chapter 21: Bond Yields (cont.)

Questions to Consider

6. Why would an investor choose bonds as an investment over stocks, especially when considering the fact that a well-chosen stock may have quite a substantial run-up in price?

    _____

    _____

    _____

    _____

7. If you buy a particular company's bond issue at face value and then learn that the same bond has been discounted by bond traders who are selling the bond at less than face value, have you lost any money?

    _____

    _____

    _____

    _____

8. What is the major drawback in buying a bond with a maturity date far into the future, 10, 20, or 30 years away?

    _____

    _____

    _____

    _____

Name: _____ Date: _____

Stocks and Bonds Crossword Puzzle

Directions: Complete the crossword puzzle using the clues below.

ACROSS

1. To stimulate stock trading, a corporation can reduce the stock price via a stock _____.
3. When ownership changes in a sole proprietorship or partnership, the life of the business _____.
6. When a stock splits, the total _____ value remains the same.
8. Ownership of a corporation comes in the form of transferable units known as shares of _____.
12. A disadvantage of preferred stock is that when profits increase, dividends remain the _____.
14. Traditional stocks have produced better _____ than other investments.
15. A benefit of being a stockholder is that your losses are limited to your _____.
17. In a sole proprietorship, the owner is subject to unlimited _____.
18. A business entity where hundreds or thousands of owners share the profits is called a _____.
19. Investors buy stock with the hope they will earn _____.

DOWN

2. Two basic types of stock are common and _____.
4. The place where stock transactions take place is called the stock _____.
5. The dividend of preferred stock is _____.
6. Corporations issue stock to raise _____.
7. A business entity where a few owners share the profits is called _____.
9. When corporations sell stock, they give up some managerial _____.
10. Dividends on preferred stock are paid _____.
11. A business entity where only one owner receives the profits is called a sole _____.
13. Americans invest more in _____ than in other investments.
16. Corporate dividends are part of the business's _____.

Section IV: Mutual Funds and Treasuries Issues

Chapter 22: Why Invest in Mutual Funds?

For those of us who lack the time and/or expertise to invest in individual stocks, an attractive option is to invest in mutual funds. Professional fund managers manage mutual funds, which is a major advantage for those who do not have the time to track stocks on a daily basis. There are over 6,000 mutual funds to choose from, and each fund has a different financial objective. A **mutual fund** consists of a large grouping of selective stocks purchased by a professional fund manager on behalf of a large group of investors.

There are mutual funds that specialize in almost anything. Some of the most familiar mutual funds specialize in growth stocks, blue chip stocks, foreign company stocks, or specific industry stocks, such as oil, gold, or agriculture. Socially responsible company stocks, such as non-tobacco/alcohol companies, or only companies that recycle or use recycled products are also some common mutual funds. Other mutual funds tend to be diverse in their investments and purchase equity in many companies, choosing a mixture of stock; thus, when one industry suffers, an opposing industry is countering and doing well, hopefully providing a consistent return.

Some of the major advantages of mutual funds would include the following:

- **Diversification** - The average individual investor usually does not have enough funding to truly achieve a diversified portfolio; that is, to have a variety of industry investments. A diversified portfolio is preferable, so that if part of the portfolio weakens, or one industry's investment slumps, the other industries' investments will compensate, giving a positive annual return.

- **Professionally Managed** - As stated earlier, if you don't have the time and/or expertise to manage your investments on a regular basis, then letting a professional manage your investments makes good sense. The professional fund manager will manage your investment and hopefully make you money; however, they do charge a fee for this service. Depending on the mutual fund and the company sponsoring the fund investment, the fees run somewhere between 1% and 8%.

- **Flexibility** - Mutual funds can be traded easily. Selling your share of a mutual fund is similar to trading stock. Sometimes you can trade one mutual fund for another at no cost. The values of mutual funds are reported in most newspapers.

- **Professional Monitoring** - Fund managers constantly monitor your mutual funds. They take care of all the buying and selling in the funds; they take care of all the paperwork; and they even prepare the records needed for tax purposes.

"I have probably purchased fifty "hot tips" in my career, maybe even more. When I put them all together, I know I am a net loser."

— Charles Schwab

Chapter 23: U.S. Treasuries

Treasuries are among the safest of all investment vehicles. With a minimum of $1,000, you can have guaranteed returns on your investment. There are several features of treasuries that make them attractive to some investors. First, they are the safest form of investment, other than a savings account, because the United States government guarantees the investment with interest. If our government fails to meet its financial obligations, you will have more important things to worry about than having your money invested in treasuries. Secondly, if you need your money now, you can sell your treasuries at any time. Thirdly, the interest you earn on treasuries is exempt from state and local taxes. Finally, if you buy your treasuries through the Federal Reserve, there are no fees involved.

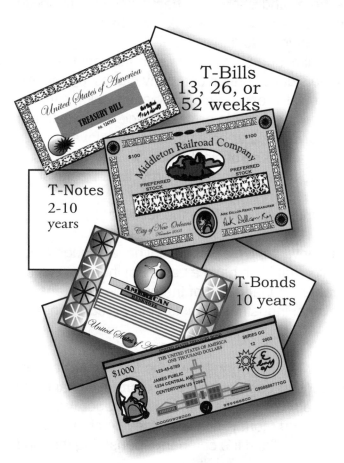

T-Bills
13, 26, or
52 weeks

T-Notes
2-10
years

T-Bonds
10 years

There are several types of treasuries that are sold by our government. The government sells treasuries in order to raise money for special projects and to meet short-term financial obligations. There are three basic types of treasuries, plus a newer vehicle that the government came out with a few years ago.

Treasury bills have maturity dates of one year or less. The maturity dates on T-bills are 13 weeks, 26 weeks, or 1 year (52 weeks). T-bills require a minimum investment of $1,000. Instead of paying interest on the $1,000, T-bills are sold at a discounted value equal to the interest that you would have earned (very similar to a U.S. Savings Bond).

Treasury notes mature in 2–10 years and require a minimum investment of $1,000. Because of the longer maturity date, treasury notes are issued at a higher interest rate than T-bills.

Treasury bonds have a maturity date of 10 years or more. Once again, because of the longer maturity rate, treasury bonds are issued at a higher interest rate. There is always a chance that interest rates will increase at an accelerated pace. If this happened, and you wanted to sell your treasury bond, it would only be bought by another if it were discounted. Treasury bonds also require a minimum investment of $1,000.

The newest version of the treasury is the **inflation-indexed note**. The U.S. government offered these bonds for the first time in January 1997. Inflation-indexed notes are similar to treasury bonds, but with a twist. Both the bond's principle and the amount of interest paid each year will increase as the consumer price index increases (adjusting for inflation).

Chapter 24: Diversification and Portfolio Management

The process of spreading your investments across assets is called **diversification**. We have all heard the old adage, "Don't put all of your eggs in one basket." What is meant by this saying is that if something would happen to cause the basket to hit the ground, then you would lose all your eggs. The same thing holds true when investing; you don't want to have all your money invested in one thing. If something would go wrong, then you might lose the vast majority of your money. Thus, you not only want to invest in several different stocks, you want to invest in many different areas, such as stocks, bonds, real estate, insurance, art, and/or precious metals (gold or silver).

There are many similar ways of describing a **portfolio**. A common factor in most definitions is to list individual investments as a **percentage** of the portfolio's total value. We call these percentages the **portfolio weights**.

For example, if we have $500 invested in stocks, $1,000 in a bond, and $2,500 in antiques, then our total portfolio would be worth $4,000. The percentage of our stock investments can be calculated by taking the value of the stocks and dividing by the total value of the portfolio, or $500 ÷ $4,000 = 12.5%. The percentage of our portfolio in the second asset is $1,000 ÷ $4,000 = 25%. The percentage of our portfolio in the third asset is $2,500 ÷ $4,000 = 62.5%. Notice that the weights have to add up to 100%, since all of our money is invested somewhere.

Two important points need to be made at this time. First, forming portfolios can eliminate some of the riskiness associated with individual assets. The principle of diversification tells us that spreading an investment across many assets will eliminate some of the risk.

The second point is equally important. There is a minimum level of risk that cannot be eliminated simply by diversifying. Diversification reduces risk, but only up to a certain point; all risk cannot be eliminated.

"90% of the people in the stock market, professionals and amateurs alike, simply haven't done enough homework."

—William J. O'Neil

Name: _____   Date: _____

Chapter 24: Diversification and Portfolio Management (cont.)

Questions for Consideration:

1. Why should diversification be a concern for all investors, especially those who may have much of their asset base invested in a single stock or a small group of closely related investments?

_____

_____

_____

2. Explain what a mutual fund is, and how it offers investors some protection against the risk of owning a single stock or a small group of stocks.

_____

_____

_____

3. Why do treasury bills, treasury notes, and treasury bonds offer investors a level of safety not available in other areas, such as stocks or corporate bonds?

_____

_____

_____

4. There are a number of different views regarding the weight that should be placed on a particular investment in an investor's overall investment portfolio. Consider the following investments: cash on deposit in a savings account, stocks, bonds, mutual funds, treasuries, and real estate. If you were investing a sum of $5,000,000, where would you put the money, and what weight would each investment carry in terms of dollar value? Be sure to explain the reasons behind the selections you made.

_____

_____

_____

_____

_____

_____

Name: _____ Date: _____

Final Evaluation

Find the simple interest earned in the following scenarios.

1. $2,500 invested for 1 year at 7.55% interest

   _____

2. $868 invested for 1 year at 3.34% interest

   _____

Determine the cost basis per share in the following scenarios.

3. 120 shares purchased at $44.20 per share, with a commission paid of $25

   _____

4. 1,500 shares purchased at $74.75 per share, with a commission paid of $125

   _____

Determine the number of shares held after the specified stock split has taken place.

5. 1,250 shares of stock, 2-for-1 split

   _____

6. 240 shares of stock, 3-for-2 split

   _____

Find the annual dividend yield in the following scenarios.

7. Stock is at $40 per share and pays a yearly dividend of $2.40.

   _____

8. Stock is at $105 per share and pays a yearly dividend of $1.10.

   _____

Use dollar cost averaging to determine the average price per share.

9. Mitchell bought 200 shares of stock in a company at $31 per share. He added another 50 shares of the same stock to his portfolio at $36.50 per share. He paid a commission of $28 on each transaction.

   _____

Final Evaluation (cont.)

10. Simone buys 20 shares of stock in a company for $120 per share, including commission. Later, she adds 25 more shares of this company's stock at a cost of $90 per share, including commission.

    _____

Determine the profit < or loss > in the following stock transactions.

11. Carlos bought 700 shares of company stock at a price of $2.40 per share, paying a commission on the purchase of $40. All shares were later sold at $2.65 per share, with a commission of $40 paid on the sale.

    _____

12. Jessica sells 20,000 shares of stock, which had a total cost of $224,800.00. The stock is sold for $14.80 per share, and a commission of $200 is paid.

    _____

Compute the price-to-earnings ratio in the following scenarios.

13. Stock price is $28.00, with earnings of $1.60.

    _____

14. Stock price is $48.50, with earnings of $2.15.

    _____

15. Stock price is $88.25, with earnings of $1.80.

    _____

Questions to Consider

Answer the following questions on your own paper.

16. What is an investment?

17. Why is dollar cost averaging a strategy used by many investors?

18. How does a wise investor balance risk with the rate of return on an investment? How does this relate to diversification?

The Stock Game

Students can play The Stock Game individually or in small teams. Small teams of two to three people usually produce more active learning. Each team should be issued the same amount of money. One team member should be designated the treasurer to keep the money and stock owned. Another student should be in charge of actually making the purchase or sale after the team members have come to complete agreement. The teacher or a small group of students can act as the exchange, where stocks are bought and sold. The choice of stocks can be any publicly held stock, or stock choices might be limited to a specific exchange, such as the NYSE or NASDAQ. Another variation is for the teacher to choose 50 to 100 stocks and limit the stock choices to only these. Typically, teachers decide on teams of two or three members. The amount of money issued needs to be a realistic amount, such as $10,000. Stock choices are usually limited to the NYSE.

The Stock Game can be played for any number of class periods or length of time. Typically, however, the game is introduced early in the semester and runs the length of the semester.

Once The Stock Game is set up, have students buy and sell stock throughout the game period with the object of making as much money as they can. Grades can be given, or at the end of the game, students could use their money to purchase prizes.

This is a great way for students to have some fun and learn about the stock market at the same time.

Included on page 53 are outlines of play money in increments of $1, $5, $10, $20, and $100. Also, there is a line on each bill for the teacher's "signature or stamp." As much money as needed can be reproduced and issued to the students. To keep students from reproducing their own money, copy the attached sheets on hard-to-find colored paper and sign each bill personally, or each bill can be stamped with a unique pattern or symbol.

Furthermore, there is a Stock Transaction Sheet (to be reproduced) located on page 52. It can be used to track each team's stock purchases, stock sales, and profits or losses.

"The important thing to recognize is that it takes a team, and the team ought to get credit for the wins and losses. Successes have many fathers, failures have none."

— Philip Caldwell

Name: _____ Date: _____

The Stock Game: Stock Transaction Sheet

Team Name _____

Team Members _____

_____

_____

_____

Date	Stock Symbol	Price Per Share	# Shares Purchased	# Shares Sold	Transaction	Profit or Loss Amt

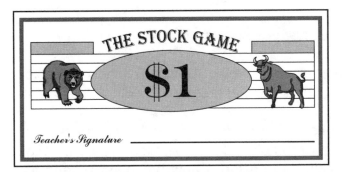

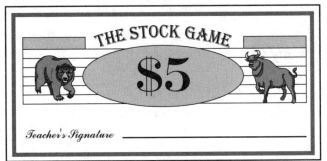

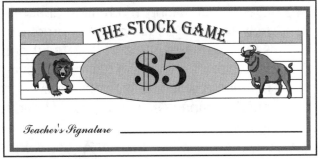

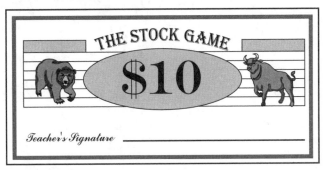

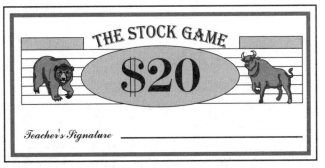

Extension Activities

Directions: Choose one or more of the following activities as a project. Developing these projects may take several class periods, and some will require additional research to complete.

1. You've just been hired by a small stock brokerage firm. Business at this company has been declining, and your job is to develop new promotional materials to entice clients to use your company's services. Your main task is to design a new brochure to send to clients, containing information about the services offered by the firm. Your boss thinks a new company logo and fresh graphics should be part of this package. One of the firm's senior partners has also told you that the company's basic messages of good research, financial planning, and steady investing need to be emphasized as well. For this activity, develop a brochure plus any other promotional materials, such as business cards, letterhead, company slogans, etc., needed to get your company's image out to clients.

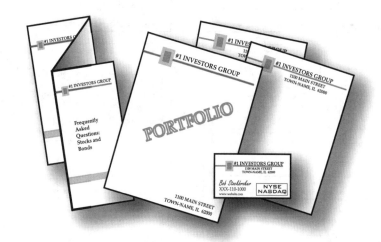

2. You've just been hired by a stock brokerage company to manage the accounts of a broker who died suddenly of heart failure at his desk. Only a few days into your new position, you find that this broker has been putting clients into very risky investments, most of which you do not agree with. This broker has also been switching client monies back and forth into different stocks simply to generate commissions for himself. (This practice is called "churning.") You find evidence that this person's approach to advising clients about investments has bordered on, or gone beyond, unethical. You've decided to call each client and inform him or her of your opinion, as well as your very different approach to managing client investments. The first client you call, however, reacts angrily to your call and your suggestions for a new approach, saying that your predecessor had previously earned him a lot of money. You don't want a repeat of this hostile call when you contact the other clients. Develop a letter or telephone script that can be used for explaining your approach to investing, with clearly stated points to highlight the advantages of your method over that of your predecessor.

Extension Activities (cont.)

3. You're a stockbroker, working at one of the larger investment houses in New York. You're having dinner at a very fine restaurant, and you overhear a faint conversation in the booth directly behind you. A doctor is telling her husband that the clinical trial of a new drug has just failed. You're familiar with this particular drug and the company that is trying to get this drug approved. You know that due to the enormous resources invested in this drug by this particular company, the company's stock price will collapse, once this news eventually gets out. Acting on this "inside" information is unethical and probably even illegal. However, you also realize that there is almost a zero percent chance of being caught if you use this information. Many of your clients are invested in this doomed stock. Write a short position paper explaining what your course of action will be, and why you have chosen that course of action.

4. The financial world has long been a subject for movies, particularly the area of financial sales. Develop a read-along play with several speaking parts that can be used to illustrate the behind-the-scenes workings of the stock trading floor of a large investment house. In writing your play, be sure to pay close attention to the different ways in which stock traders might speak to each other during the course of the day, and how that differs from the language they use with clients. Also, pay attention to the story line you select. A good play needs to fully develop the characters involved and convey a plot appropriate to the characters and setting.

5. This activity will take you into the world of financial reporting. You'll need to watch several financial news-related broadcasts, check websites that report financial news, and review printed sources, such as newspapers and magazines that are devoted to financial reporting. Write a short synopsis of each medium you observed, describing the manner in which the financial news is reported. You'll begin to see differences in the way stories are handled, once you become familiar with the different news providers. You may want to organize the information you've collected into a table or chart for easier reference. Pay special attention to the following: What is the format of each media outlet that makes it different from its competitors? Which outlets provide continuous coverage? How does the coverage of news in a monthly magazine differ from a daily news broadcast? Which outlets offered opinions regarding the news they were covering? Did you see any bias in the reporting of stories? Did any of the publications appear to be promoting or hyping a particular company's stock?

6. What do people think about investing? This activity will give you a look at how people invest their money and their views on investing. Compose three to five questions for a survey, and log people's responses. Possible survey questions: What is the single investment you trust most? If you invest in stocks, how many times did you buy or sell stocks during the past year? Do you trust corporations to give honest financial information? Once your survey has been completed, prepare a table, and write a short summary to explain the responses.

Glossary of Frequently Used Financial Terms

Bears and Bulls: Animal mascots used for describing market activity. Bears are associated with a downward market. Bulls represent a rising market.

Blue Chip Stock: Term used to describe the stocks of large, well-established companies whose size, stability, and profitability make owning these stocks less risky.

Bond: An investor may purchase a bond in much the same way as buying stocks. It is essentially a loan made to a company by an investor. The bond is a contract made by the company to pay the investor a fixed amount of money when the bond matures (when the loan term ends). Companies sometimes issue bonds instead of trying to borrow money from banks, since the interest rates paid on bonds are ordinarily lower than interest on a loan made by a bank. A **Convertible Bond** is a special kind of bond that may be converted into company stock. See also **Municipal Bond** and **Junk Bond**.

Buy and Hold: Term used to describe the strategy of buying stocks of quality companies, then holding those stocks over a long period of time. Most buy and hold strategies involve stocks that pay dividends.

Commission: A fee paid to a broker or brokerage house by an investor for making stock trades on the investor's behalf. People who trade stocks using a computer are actually going through a brokerage with those transactions.

Cost Basis: With a stock purchase, this is the amount of money paid for stock(s) when both the price paid per share and commission paid are computed.

Day Trading: Term used to describe the strategy of trading in and out of stocks during a given trading day, in order to realize profits on tiny price increases. Most day traders prefer to hold few (or no) stocks at the end of a trading day.

Diversify: Simply means to split your investment monies between different stocks, or into different investment vehicles, such as real estate, stocks, bonds, etc. The idea behind diversification is that if you have invested in many different areas, then a failure of a single investment doesn't wipe out all of your assets at once.

Glossary of Frequently Used Financial Terms (cont.)

Dividend: A payment made by a company to shareholders for owning shares of company stock. Dividends are set amounts, usually paid by the company each quarter. Typically, a dividend payment represents about 1% to 5% of the amount at which the stock itself trades.

Dollar Cost Averaging: Many investors buy the stock of a company they like over a period of time, realizing in advance that the price per share is likely to fluctuate. Dollar cost averaging allows the average price per share to be computed for investors who may buy a particular stock at different price levels.

Interest: This is a percentage amount paid by a bank or other financial institution to investors for money deposited with that institution. Most savings, checking, and brokerage accounts pay interest in some form.

Investment: Money put into either a tangible item or a financial instrument for the purpose of increasing the original amount of money.

Junk Bond: Issued by a company with a low rating for credit worthiness. Some investors buy "junk," due to the high interest rate paid by the company to induce investors to buy these bonds. Where there is high interest offered, there is usually high risk to go with it. Some junk bonds never return the original investment, due to company default or bankruptcy.

Margin Buying: This is a strategy that involves borrowing money against your portfolio in order to buy more shares of stock. This works well in a rising market. Margin calls take place when prices decline, and the brokerage house requires stocks to be sold or additional monies to be placed into the brokerage account.

Municipal Bond: Issued by a state or city government, usually to pay for a particular public works project. These bonds are favored by investors since the chance of default is perceived as being small. Sometimes these bonds are tax-free as well. Often called "Munis."

Mutual Fund: Large stock portfolios where many investors have pooled their money to purchase stocks. Typically, a fund manager makes decisions about buying and selling the fund's holdings.

Portfolio: A group of stocks held by an individual or investment group.

Price-to-Earnings Ratio or **P/E:** A commonly used assessment for gauging a stock's value, based on its price and earnings.

Profit or **Net Profit:** This is the amount of money an investment has earned after the total cost of the investment has been considered. Part of the cost of an investment is fees or expenses incurred as a result of making the investment.

Glossary of Frequently Used Financial Terms (cont.)

Rate of Return: This is essentially the amount of profit, typically expressed as a percentage rate, that an investment is expected to pay.

Risk or **Risk Tolerance:** Investments are made in the hope of earning a profit on the investment. Safer investments, such as bank savings accounts, typically offer very small interest payments as a rate of return. A very risky investment might offer a very high rate of return, but for that high rate of return, the investor risks losing some (or all) of the investment.

Short or **Short Sell:** A strategy that involves borrowing shares of stock, usually through a brokerage house, and selling those shares at the current price. Short sellers make a profit if the price of the stock declines, since they can replace the borrowed shares at a lower price. When a stock price rises, though, the shorts must scramble to cover the borrowed stock, often at much higher prices.

Stock: Shares of stock are essentially small pieces of ownership in a company that are available for purchase. The larger companies have many millions of shares of stock outstanding. Many companies therefore have thousands of owners.

Stock Split: Occurs when shares of stock in a company are multiplied according to an announced ratio.

Stock Index: Groups a number of stocks together in order to track their progress as a group. Generally, if most stocks are rising, then the index rises. Likewise, if most stocks in an index are declining, then so will the index. An index provides a quick and convenient way to gauge how the market is doing, without having to check the price of dozens (or hundreds) of individual stocks.

Treasuries: Treasury bills, notes, and bonds issued by the U.S. government. These are considered a safe investment, but accordingly, the interest rate paid is modest when compared to some investments.

Yield: Percentage rate of actual return on a particular investment. For instance, "dividend yield" refers to the percentage of return a particular dividend represents in relation to the price of the stock itself.

USEFUL FORMULAS—To calculate ...
- **Simple Interest:** Interest Rate x Principal = Interest Earned
- **Total Cost of Shares:** Number of Shares x Price of Shares + Commission paid = Total Cost of Shares
- **Cost Basis Per Share:** Total Cost ÷ Number of Shares Bought = Cost Basis Per Share
- **Dividend Yield of a Stock:** Dividend ÷ Stock Price = Yield
- **Earnings Per Share:** Net Income ÷ Total Shares Outstanding = EPS
- **Price to Earnings (P/E Ratio):** Price Per Share ÷ EPS = P/E Ratio
- **Dollar Cost Averaging:** Total Cost ÷ Total Number of Shares = Average Price Per Share
- **Bond Yield:** Coupon ÷ Price = Yield (%)

Answer Keys

A Quick Overview of Investing (pages 3–4)

1. Probably not. Most loans made to friends are without interest (without profit), and therefore not an investment.
2. Yes. The $10,000 was invested with the view of using that starter money to earn even more money with a business. If the money was lost, obviously it wasn't a good investment.
3. Most people want to be able to readily get their money out of an investment, if a need for the money arises.
4. Certainly many factors affect the value of an antique car, and such a car may be very difficult to sell at its true fair value. A savings account is a very safe investment, and it requires no specialized knowledge.
5. Since 200 more copies of this musician's autograph will soon be available, you should expect the price of yours to plummet.
6. Not necessarily. Many things determine the value of a company's stock beyond the product they make. It could be that this company makes an excellent product, but their cost of making that product may be too high to ever make a profit.
7. Yes. Stocks are a very good example. When the economy is good, and economic conditions look promising, sometimes the value of a company's stock will rise well beyond its actual worth. Likewise, if news is bad, people may panic and sell stocks, causing stock prices to tumble. The feeling that investors have is often referred to as "investor sentiment."
8. Answers will vary. Basic questions concerning the risk involved, rate of return on the investment, and length of time in which the investment will be made are likely.

Using Financial Terms (page 5–6)

1. investment
2. stock
3. interest
4. cost basis
5. junk bond
6. treasuries
7. dividend
8. day trading
9. mutual fund
10. dollar cost averaging
11. stock index
12. margin buying
13. commission
14. diversification
15. risk
16. short sell

Banks and Simple Interest (page 9)

1. $9.86
2. $178
3. $136,000
4. $2,289.50
5. $2,350
6. $40
7. $7,328.75

Common and Preferred Stock (page 13)

1.

Distribution	First Year	Second Year	Third Year
Preferred:	$5,000	$5,000	$4,000
Common:	$10,000	$20,000	$0
Dividend Per Share			
Preferred:	$5	$5	$4
Common:	$2	$4	$0

2. | **Distribution** | **First Year** | **Second Year** | **Third Year** |
|---|---|---|---|
| Preferred: | $8,000 | $8,000 | $8,000 |
| Common: | $12,000 | $27,000 | $52,000 |
| **Dividend Per Share** | | | |
| Preferred: | $8 | $8 | $8 |
| Common: | $3 | $6.75 | $13 |

Stock Purchases and Cost Basis (pages 15–16)

1. $1,156.00
2. $4,265.00
3. $18.84
4. $26.81
5. $16,625.00, $55.42
6. $113.00, $11.30
7. $11,975.00, $23.95
8. $155,237.50, $30.59
9. $22,200.00, $1.11
10. $12,845.00, $98.81
11. $3,440.00, $34.40
12. The commission paid tends to have a smaller effect on cost basis when dealing with larger blocks of stock. This is because the cost of the commission is spread out over a greater number of shares.
13. If you make many stock trades per day or per month, then the cost of each trade becomes a greater factor in terms of total cost of the stocks acquired. An investor who makes fewer stock purchases, perhaps in larger blocks, feels the commission bite far less than a frequent trader.

Stock Splits (page 20)

1. 1,800,000
2. 225
3. 20,000
4. 6,000
5. 5
6. 4 for 1

Dividend Yield (pages 22–23)

1. 5%
2. 3%
3. 3.73%
4. 12.5%
5. 4%
6. 6.67%
7. 0.85%
8. 11.5%
9. 2.92%
10. 9.17%
11. 0.22%
12. 2.06%

Price-to-Earnings Ratio (pages 31–32)

1. 16.67
2. 7.89
3. 37.50
4. 23.03
5. 3
6. 24.25
7. 7
8. P/E ratio gives different information from dividend yield. A high P/E might be a warning that the stock is more vulnerable to decline.
9. Answers will vary. Debt load, basic business model, company leadership, and economic conditions all exert influence on the success of a company.
10. Some investors see a decline (even a minor one) in earnings as very bad news and will flee from stocks with such earnings setbacks. Many investors choose to weather such setbacks, especially if they are only temporary, and are rewarded for the effort.
11. This is often the case. Rising earnings make a company look more attractive to investors. As the stock price rises, dividend yield will decrease unless the dividend is raised to keep up with the increasing stock price. From this example, you can see how many of these company financial numbers are intertwined with one another.

Another Look at Cost Basis (page 33)
1. $7,705.00   2. $4.41   3. $4,485.00   4. $19.23   5. $10.37
6. $8.33 (The shares were a gift; therefore, the commission was the only cost for the shares.)

Dollar Cost Averaging (pages 34–35)
1. $104.20   2. $11.96   3. $111.62   4. $42.88   5. $11.79
6. Since it is very difficult to accurately predict the low for a given stock, many investors feel that dollar cost averaging provides good protection against the risk of investing all of one's funds when the stock price might be at its highest.
7. Commissions being paid on multiple purchases is a major drawback, especially if the lots of stock bought are small. In this scenario, commissions will tend to greatly increase the average price paid per share.

Another Look at Dollar Cost Averaging (page 36)
1. $2.62   2. $44.17   3. $26.76   4. $24.18
5. Dollar cost averaging can work for an investor who sells some shares at a loss, as long as more shares are sold at a profit. That's why the average price per share becomes an important factor in making sell decisions.
6. It makes no sense to accumulate a stock if you have reason to believe that the price is declining with little hope of rebound. There will be no profits to balance the losses. The old saying, "Throwing good money after bad" would seem to apply.

Stock Sales (page 37–38)
1. $400.00   2. $1,883.00   3. < $261.25 >   4. $17,270.00
5. < $1.50 >   6. $55,710.00   7. < $1,070.50 >

Another Look at Stock Sales (page 39)
1. $7,903.00   2. $310.75   3. < $181.00 >   4. $391.10
5. $2,628.00   6. $31,500.00

Bond Yields (pages 42–43)
1. 3.43%   2. 12.21%   3. 14.75%   4. 8.98%   5. 11.62%
6. In general, bonds are a safer investment than stocks, and the return on a bond investment is known in advance. The uncertainty of stocks, therefore, makes bonds more attractive to many investors.
7. No. You still own the bond at the price you paid, and are owed the interest you were promised. However, other investors have the opportunity to get into the same investment you have, now at a lesser cost. That's how investing works sometimes.
8. Bonds of this length represent a commitment that is sometimes imprudent in an ever-changing economic world. Better financial opportunities may pop up while you are still holding this long-term bond issue. What if you buy a bond with a 2% coupon, and interest rates later skyrocket to 20%?

Stocks and Bonds Crossword Puzzle (page 44)

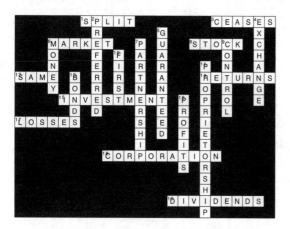

Diversification and Portfolio Management (page 48)

1. Unexpected turns in economic conditions can wreak havoc on investors who have too much of their asset base alloted too narrowly. A recent example of this was a large energy company that went bankrupt, with many employees having their entire retirement fund invested in the company's stock.
2. Mutual funds are simply large portfolios where investors pool their monies. Usually, these funds are professionally managed, and there is a little more risk protection for the investor over holding individual stocks. As witnessed in recent years, though, even mutual funds can decline in value during downward markets.
3. These instruments are backed by the U.S. government.
4. Answers will vary. The purpose of this question is for students to weigh each investment and apply some of the knowledge they have regarding diversification and the power of interest-yielding investments.

Final Evaluation (pages 49–50)

1. $188.75
2. $28.99
3. $44.40
4. $74.83
5. 2,500
6. 360
7. 6%
8. 1.05%
9. $32.32
10. $103.33
11. $95.00
12. $71,000.00
13. 17.5
14. 22.56
15. 49.03
16. Money put into a tangible item or financial instrument for the purpose of increasing that original amount of money.
17. It allows investors to buy stocks at different times at different price levels and still be able to compute an average cost for shares. It assists with making decisions about selling the stock, acquiring more shares, etc.
18. Investors must always balance the rewards of high returns against the risk of an investment. In general, a riskier investment pays a higher rate of return in order to attract investing capital. Diversification keeps the investor spread out over many different investments and, therefore, protected to a reasonable extent from being ruined by only one or two failed investments.

Extension Activities (pages 54–55)

Answers will vary.